'IT IS NOT WHAT GOES INTO THE MOUTH OF A MAN
THAT DEFILES AND DISHONORS HIM, BUT WHAT
COMES OUT OF THE MOUTH, THIS DEFILES AND
DISHONORS HIM.'

BY BILL AMOR

'IT IS NOT WHAT GOES INTO THE MOUTH OF A MAN THAT DEFILES AND DISHONORS HIM, BUT WHAT COMES OUT OF THE MOUTH, THIS DEFILES AND DISHONORS HIM.'

written by Bill Amor

1st Edition © 2026 by Bill Amor

ISBN: 979-8-9945805-0-9

Scripture quotations taken from the KING JAMES VERSION (KJV): KING JAMES VERSION, public domain.

Scripture quotations taken from the Amplified® Bible, Copyright © 1954, 1958, 1962, 1964, 1965, 1987 by The Lockman Foundation. Used by permission. All rights reserved

About Apostle Bill Amor

Apostle Bill Amor's life is a testament to the power of faith, perseverance, and divine intervention. Diagnosed with autism as a child and considered high-functioning as an adult, Apostle Amor has faced challenges that would have broken many. Born into a world that often misunderstood him, young Bill struggled with feelings of isolation and inadequacy. Despite these challenges, he displayed remarkable determination. At the age of 12, he achieved a significant milestone by winning a reading competition—an accomplishment that filled him with pride and optimism. However, this joy was short-lived when his mother tearfully shared devastating news from the doctor: he was not expected to live beyond the age of 28 to 32. This revelation shattered his world.

Overwhelmed by fear and hopelessness, Bill sought solace in his best friend John Straw, only to discover that John had been taken away by his brother Andy. Feeling abandoned and consumed by anger, he fled into the woods near his home. It was there, amidst the trees and shadows of doubt, that he cried out to God in desperation. Bill's life changed forever on that fateful day. As he climbed a steep hill toward his neighbor's house, he encountered what can only be described as a divine vision: Jesus Christ Himself appeared before him at the top of the hill near a chain-link fence.

The image was vivid—Jesus stood before him with pockmarks where His beard had been removed and glistening divots on His cheeks and chin. He did not resemble traditional depictions; instead, He appeared timeless yet distinct from modern trends. This miraculous encounter marked the beginning of Apostle Amor's transformation. From a young boy who felt lost and unworthy, he grew into a man devoted to spreading God's message of love and repentance. Through trials and tribulations—including struggles with literacy —he found strength in faith and discovered his purpose as an apostle.

TABLE OF CONTENTS

Summary of Apostle Bill Amor's Teaching Based on Matthew 15:11 (AMP Version)

To summarize the teaching of Apostle Bill Amor based on Matthew 15:11 in the Amplified Bible (AMP) version, we must first understand the context and meaning of this verse. The verse states:

"It is not what goes into the mouth of a man that defiles and dishonors him, but what comes out of the mouth, this defiles and dishonors him."

This statement by Jesus was made during a debate with Jewish leaders about ceremonial handwashing and dietary laws. Below is a step-by-step breakdown to provide clarity:

Step 1: Context of Matthew 15:11

In this passage, Jesus addresses the Pharisees and scribes who criticized His disciples for eating without following traditional handwashing rituals. These religious leaders equated external cleanliness with spiritual purity. However, Jesus challenges their focus on outward actions rather than inward morality.

Step 2: Key Message in Matthew 15:11

Jesus emphasizes that true defilement does not come from external sources like food or unwashed hands but from internal sources such as thoughts, words, and intentions. He explains that what comes out of a person's mouth reflects their heart's condition. Evil thoughts, slander, lies, and other sinful behaviors originate from within and are what truly dishonor a person before God.

Step 3: Explanation of Defilement

Jesus elaborates further in verses Matthew 15:17-20, explaining that food passes through the body and is eliminated. In contrast, words spoken reveal deeper issues rooted in the heart—such as evil intentions, hatred, or deceit—which lead to spiritual impurity. This teaching shifts the focus from ritualistic practices to moral integrity.

Step 4: Spiritual Implications

The teaching underscores that God judges individuals based on their hearts rather than external actions alone. While outward rituals may have symbolic value, they do not determine one's holiness or righteousness before God. Instead, it is essential to cultivate pure motives and avoid harboring negative emotions or intentions.

Conclusion

Apostle Bill Amor's teaching likely highlights that true spirituality involves self-reflection on one's inner life rather than adherence to external traditions or rituals. Words spoken reflect the state of one's heart;

therefore, believers must strive for purity in thought and speech to honor God genuinely.

Introduction

"It is not what goes into the mouth of a man that defiles and dishonors him, but what comes out of the mouth, this defiles and dishonors him" (Matthew 15:11, AMP). This profound statement by Jesus Christ challenges traditional notions of purity and holiness, shifting the focus from external rituals to the internal condition of the heart. In this teaching, Apostle Bill Amor delves deeply into the meaning and implications of this verse, emphasizing its relevance for modern believers. By addressing the importance of words as reflections of one's inner character, he highlights how true spirituality is not determined by outward actions or ceremonial practices but by the moral integrity and intentions that govern our lives. This introduction sets the stage for exploring how Jesus' message calls us to examine our hearts and align our speech with godly principles.

Chapter 1: The Heart of Defilement

The core message of Matthew 15:11 is that defilement is not about external rituals or physical consumption, but about what originates from within a person's heart. This teaching by Jesus directly challenges traditional Jewish views on ceremonial cleanliness, shifting the focus from outward actions to inward intentions and moral character.

Step 1: Contextual Background of Matthew 15:11

To understand the significance of Matthew 15:11, it is essential to first consider the cultural and religious context in which Jesus spoke these words. During this time, Jewish religious leaders, particularly the Pharisees and scribes, placed great emphasis on ceremonial laws and traditions. These included practices such as ritual handwashing before meals, which were seen as necessary for maintaining spiritual purity. While these traditions were not explicitly commanded in Scripture, they had become deeply ingrained in Jewish religious life.

The Pharisees believed that failing to observe these rituals could render a person spiritually unclean or defiled. Their concern was rooted in a strict interpretation of Levitical laws regarding cleanliness (e.g., Leviticus 11). However, Jesus challenged this perspective by asserting that true defilement does not come from external sources—such as eating with unwashed hands—but rather from what comes out of a person's mouth, which reflects the condition of their heart.

Step 2: Jesus' Radical Teaching

In Matthew 15:11, Jesus declares, "Not what goes into the mouth defiles a man; but what comes out of the mouth, this defiles a man." This statement was revolutionary because it overturned long-held beliefs about purity and holiness. By emphasizing internal morality over external rituals, Jesus shifted the focus from legalistic adherence to traditions toward the deeper issue of inner righteousness.

Jesus' teaching highlights two key points:

External actions are not inherently defiling: Eating certain foods or neglecting ritual handwashing does not make a person spiritually impure. These are physical acts that have no bearing on one's moral standing before God.

The heart as the source of defilement: What truly defiles a person is what originates from within—their thoughts, intentions, and words. As Jesus explains later in Matthew 15:18–19, "But those things which proceed out of the mouth come from

the heart, and they defile a man. For out of the heart proceed evil thoughts, murders, adulteries, fornications, thefts, false witness, blasphemies."

Step 3: Challenging Traditional Views

By making this statement, Jesus directly confronted the Pharisees' reliance on human traditions to define spiritual purity. In Matthew 15:3–9, He rebuked them for prioritizing man-made rules over God's commandments. He quoted Isaiah's prophecy to expose their hypocrisy: "These people honor me with their lips, but their hearts are far from me" (Matthew 15:8).

This critique underscores an important theme in Jesus' ministry: authentic worship and righteousness must come from the heart rather than mere outward conformity to religious practices. The Pharisees' obsession with external cleanliness blinded them to their own inner corruption.

Step 4: Implications for Modern Readers

The message of Matthew 15:11 remains relevant today as it challenges individuals to examine their own hearts and motivations rather than focusing solely on outward appearances or behaviors. It calls for self-reflection and an honest assessment of one's inner life.

Modern applications include:

Recognizing that true spirituality is rooted in love for God and others rather than rigid adherence to rituals or traditions.

Understanding that harmful words and actions stem from deeper issues within the heart.

Seeking transformation through repentance and renewal by God's grace.

In conclusion, Chapter 1 introduces readers to the profound truth at the heart of Matthew 15:11—that spiritual purity is determined not by external factors, but by what resides within us. By addressing this fundamental issue, Jesus invites His followers to pursue genuine righteousness that flows from a transformed heart.

Chapter 2: Words That Build or Destroy

Introduction: The Power of Words

In Matthew 15:11, Jesus states, "It is not what goes into the mouth that defiles a person, but what comes out of the mouth; this defiles a person." This profound statement shifts the focus from external rituals to internal character and highlights the immense power of our words. Words are not merely sounds or symbols; they are reflections of our hearts and have the ability to build up or destroy. As Proverbs 18:21 declares, "Death and life are in the power of the tongue, and those who love it will eat its fruits." This chapter explores how words reveal our inner nature and their potential to impact others positively or negatively.

The Reflection of Inner Character

Words serve as a mirror to our inner selves. Jesus emphasized this connection in Matthew 12:34 when He said, "Out of the abundance of the heart the mouth speaks." Similarly, Proverbs 10:11 describes how "The mouth of the righteous is a fountain of life," while "the mouth of the wicked conceals violence." These verses illustrate that speech is not an isolated act but a direct expression of one's moral and spiritual state.

When we speak kind, encouraging words, it reflects a heart filled with goodness and wisdom. Conversely, harsh or deceitful words reveal bitterness, anger, or malice within. This principal underscores why controlling our speech is so critical—not just for interpersonal relationships but also as evidence of our spiritual health.

Words That Destroy

The destructive potential of words cannot be overstated. Proverbs 12:18 warns that "There is one whose rash words are like sword thrusts," vividly illustrating how careless speech can wound others deeply. Gossip, slander, lies, and insults are all examples of verbal weapons that can harm reputations, sever relationships, and even lead to long-term emotional scars.

James 3:6 compares the tongue to a fire capable of setting an entire forest ablaze. This metaphor captures how unchecked speech can escalate conflicts and cause widespread damage. Hurtful words often leave lasting impressions on those who hear them—sometimes shaping their self-perception for years to come.

Moreover, destructive speech does not only harm others; it also harms the speaker. Proverbs 10:19 notes that "When words are many, transgression is not lacking," highlighting how excessive or unrestrained talking often leads to sin. Those who fail to guard their tongues risk losing credibility and respect within their communities.

Words That Build

On the other hand, words have incredible potential to heal and uplift. Proverbs 16:24 beautifully states that "Gracious words are like a honeycomb, sweetness to the soul and health to the body." Encouraging someone with kind remarks can brighten their day or even change their outlook on life entirely.

Healing words include honesty spoken with love (Proverbs 27:5-6), calm responses that diffuse anger (Proverbs 15:1), timely advice (Proverbs 15:23), and affirmations that bring hope (Proverbs 12:25). These types of speech foster trust, strengthen relationships, and promote emotional well-being.

For example, consider how meaningful compliments or expressions of gratitude can transform someone's mood. A simple acknowledgment like "I appreciate your hard work" can motivate individuals to continue striving for excellence. Similarly, offering forgiveness through sincere apologies has immense power to mend broken bonds.

Practical Steps for Speaking Life

To consistently use words that build rather than destroy requires intentionality:

Guard Your Heart: Since speech flows from what resides in our hearts (Luke 6:45), cultivating virtues such as kindness, patience, and humility is essential.

Think Before You Speak: Proverbs 15:28 advises that "The heart of the righteous ponders how to answer." Taking time to reflect before speaking prevents impulsive remarks.

Practice Restraint: As Proverbs 17:28 notes, even fools appear wise when they remain silent.

Seek Divine Help: Changing harmful speech patterns ultimately requires God's intervention through prayer and reliance on His Spirit (Psalm 141:3).

By following these steps—and relying on God's grace—we can ensure our words consistently reflect His love and truth

Conclusion

Matthew 15:11 reminds us that what comes out of our mouths holds far greater significance than external actions because it reveals who we truly are inside. Our words possess tremendous power; they can either build up or tear down those around us while simultaneously reflecting our inner character.

As followers of Christ called to be His representatives on earth (Colossians 3:17), we must strive daily toward using language that glorifies Him by bringing life rather than death into every conversation we engage in.

"Death and life are in the power of the tongue"—may we always choose life!

Chapter 3: Traditions vs. Truth

In Matthew 15:11, Jesus declares, "Not what goes into the mouth defiles a man; but what comes out of the mouth, this defiles a man." This profound statement lies at the heart of His confrontation with the Pharisees and scribes, exposing their misplaced priorities and their elevation of human traditions above God's commandments. This chapter will explore how Jesus challenged these religious leaders, the implications for modern believers, and how we too can avoid falling into similar traps by prioritizing rituals over genuine faith.

The Context of Matthew 15:11

The confrontation in Matthew 15 begins when the Pharisees and scribes accuse Jesus' disciples of breaking "the tradition of the elders" by eating without ceremonially washing their hands (Matthew 15:1-2). This ceremonial washing was not a commandment from God but rather a tradition developed by Jewish leaders to ensure ritual purity. While it may have had practical or symbolic value, it was not rooted in Scripture.

Jesus responds sharply by pointing out that these religious leaders were guilty of something far worse: they transgressed God's commandments in order to uphold their traditions (Matthew 15:3). He provides an example where they used a tradition—declaring possessions as "Corban" (dedicated to God)—to avoid helping their parents, thereby violating the fifth commandment to honor father and mother (Matthew 15:4-6). By doing so, they nullified God's Word for the sake of human rules.

This sets the stage for Jesus' revolutionary teaching in Matthew 15:11. He shifts the focus from external rituals to internal realities, stating that true defilement comes not from what enters the body but from what proceeds out of one's heart through words and actions.

The Pharisees' Misplaced Priorities

The Pharisees' obsession with external cleanliness reflected a broader problem: they prioritized outward appearances over inward transformation. Their traditions emphasized strict adherence to rules about food, washing, and other ceremonial practices while neglecting matters of the heart.

Jesus quotes Isaiah 29:13 to expose their hypocrisy: "These people draw near to Me with their mouth, and honor Me with their lips, but their heart is far from Me" (Matthew 15:8). Their worship was superficial because it was based on human doctrines rather than divine truth.

By focusing on external rituals, they missed the deeper issue—sin originates in the heart. As Jesus later explains to His disciples in Matthew 15:18-19, evil thoughts such as murder, adultery, thefts, false witness, and blasphemies come from within. These are what truly defile a person—not whether someone eats with unwashed hands.

Modern Parallels: When Rituals Replace Faith

The tendency to prioritize human traditions over God's Word is not limited to first-century Pharisees; it remains a challenge for modern believers as well. Many Christians today may fall into similar traps by emphasizing rituals or outward displays of religiosity while neglecting genuine faith and obedience.

Examples of Modern-Day Traditions

Legalism in Worship Practices -
Some churches elevate specific styles of worship music or liturgical practices as though they are divinely mandated. While these traditions may hold cultural or historical significance, they should never overshadow biblical principles like love for God and neighbor.

Ritualistic Observance Without Heart Engagement
Participating in sacraments such as baptism or communion

without understanding their spiritual significance can reduce them to empty rituals. True worship requires heartfelt devotion rather than mere formalism.

Cultural Christianity -
In some contexts, being a Christian is more about adhering to social norms or family traditions than cultivating a personal relationship with Christ. This can lead to nominal faith that lacks transformative power.

Judging Others Based on External Standards -
Just as the Pharisees judged others for failing to follow ceremonial washings, modern Christians sometimes judge fellow believers based on dress codes or dietary choices rather than focusing on matters of character and faithfulness.

The Danger of Elevating Tradition Above Scripture

When human traditions are elevated above Scripture:

God's Commandments Are Neglected -
Just as the Pharisees neglected honoring their parents due to Corban vows (Matthew 15:5-6), modern believers risk sidelining clear biblical commands when traditions take precedence.

Worship Becomes Vain -
Jesus warns that worship rooted in human doctrines is futile (Matthew 15:9). True worship must be grounded in spirit and truth (John 4:24).

Spiritual Blindness Develops -
Jesus describes the Pharisees as "blind leaders of the blind" who lead others into destruction (Matthew 15:14). Similarly, clinging stubbornly to man-made rules can prevent individuals from seeing God's truth clearly.

Guarding Against Ritualism Today

To avoid falling into the trap of prioritizing tradition over truth:

Examine Your Heart Regularly -

Reflect on whether your actions stem from genuine love for God or merely adherence to routine.

Prioritize Scripture Over Human Rules -
Measure all teachings and practices against God's Word rather than blindly following cultural norms or church customs.

Focus on Internal Transformation -
Remember that true holiness begins in the heart (Matthew 15:18-19). Seek God's help through prayer and study to cultivate purity within.

Extend Grace Toward Others -
Avoid judging others based on non-essential matters like food choices or worship styles (Romans 14). Instead, encourage one another toward love and good deeds (Hebrews 10:24).

Conclusion

In Matthew 15:11, Jesus challenges us to rethink our understanding of spiritual defilement by shifting our focus from external rituals to internal realities. His confrontation with the Pharisees serves as both a warning against elevating human traditions above God's commandments and an invitation to pursue authentic faith rooted in love for God and neighbor. As modern believers navigate questions about tradition versus truth today, we must remain vigilant against legalism while striving for hearts transformed by grace—a transformation that manifests not only in our words but also in our actions toward others.

Chapter 4: The Power of Words – What Comes Out of the Mouth Defiles

Introduction: Understanding Matthew 15:11

Matthew 15:11 states, "Not what goes into the mouth defiles a man; but what comes out of the mouth, this defiles a man." This verse is a profound teaching by Jesus that shifts the focus from external rituals to internal morality. In this chapter, we will explore how words reflect the condition of the heart and their power to either build or destroy. We will also connect this teaching to other scriptures and examine its relevance in modern life.

The Context of Matthew 15:11

To fully grasp the meaning of Matthew 15:11, it is essential to understand its context. Jesus was addressing the Pharisees and scribes who criticized His disciples for not following traditional handwashing rituals before eating (Matthew 15:1-2). These traditions were not part of God's law but were human-made rules elevated to divine status by religious leaders.

Jesus responded by pointing out their hypocrisy, accusing them of prioritizing human traditions over God's commandments (Matthew 15:3-6). He then declared that true defilement does not come from external sources like unwashed hands or food but from within—specifically, from what comes out of a person's mouth.

This statement was revolutionary because it challenged the prevailing Jewish understanding of purity laws. It emphasized internal righteousness over external compliance with ceremonial practices.

Words as a Reflection of the Heart

Jesus' teaching in Matthew 15:11 highlights that words are not merely sounds; they are expressions of what resides in our hearts. In Matthew 12:34-35, Jesus elaborates on this idea, saying, "For out of the abundance of the heart the mouth speaks. A good man out of the good treasure of his heart brings forth good things, and an evil man out of the evil treasure brings forth evil things."

This connection between words and the heart underscores that our speech reveals our true character. If our hearts are filled with love, kindness, and truth, our words will reflect those qualities. Conversely, if our hearts harbor hatred, bitterness, or deceit, these will manifest in our speech.

Real-Life Application:

Consider how often careless words lead to conflict or pain. Gossip can ruin reputations; harsh criticism can damage relationships; lies can erode trust. On the other hand, kind words can heal wounds, encourage others, and foster unity.

Proverbs 18:21 reinforces this concept by stating, "Death and life are in the power of the tongue." This verse reminds us that our words have immense power; they can either bring life or cause destruction.

Biblical Examples Illustrating the Power of Words

The Bible provides numerous examples demonstrating how words can either glorify God or lead to sin:

Positive Example – King David's Psalms:
David frequently used his words to praise God and express his faith (e.g., Psalm 23). His psalms continue to inspire believers today because they reflect a heart devoted to God.

Negative Example – The Israelites' Complaints:
In Exodus 16:2-3 and Numbers 14:1-4, we see how the Israelites' grumbling against God led to judgment. Their complaints revealed their lack of faith and gratitude despite God's provision.

Jesus' Words on Forgiveness:

In Luke 23:34, as Jesus hung on the cross, He said, "Father, forgive them; for they know not what they do." These words exemplify grace and mercy even in suffering.

These examples illustrate that words have consequences —they can either align with God's will or oppose it

Practical Steps for Guarding Our Speech

Given the importance Jesus places on what comes out of our mouths in Matthew 15:11, how can we ensure that our speech honors God? Here are some practical steps:

Examine Your Heart -
Since words flow from what is in our hearts (Matthew 12:34), it is crucial to regularly examine our thoughts and attitudes. Are there areas where bitterness or pride has taken root? Confess these sins to God and ask Him to purify your heart (Psalm 51:10).

Meditate on Scripture -
Filling your mind with God's Word helps transform your heart and influences your speech positively (Romans 12:2). Memorize verses like Ephesians 4:29— "Let no corrupt word proceed out of your mouth..."

Practice Self-Control -
James 1:19 advises believers to be "quick to listen," "slow to speak," and "slow to anger." Before speaking impulsively, pause and consider whether your words will build up or tear down.

Seek Accountability -
Surround yourself with fellow believers who can lovingly correct you when your speech does not align with Christ-like behavior (Proverbs 27:17).

Pray for Wisdom -
Ask God for wisdom in choosing your words carefully (James 1:5). Pray daily for guidance so that your speech reflects His love and truth.

Connecting Matthew 15:11 with Modern Life

In today's world—dominated by social media—words carry even greater weight because they reach wider audiences instantly. Online platforms often amplify negativity through gossiping posts or hateful comments. As Christians living in such an environment:

Reflect Christ-like humility online.

Avoid engaging in divisive arguments.

Use digital spaces as opportunities for encouragement rather than criticism.

Additionally:

Consider workplace conversations where gossip may arise.

Think about family dynamics where harsh tones might escalate conflicts unnecessarily. By applying principles derived from Matthew Chapter Fifteen Verse Eleven consistently across all areas—including digital interactions —we demonstrate obedience towards Christ-centered living rooted deeply inwardly rather than externally superficiality-driven motives!

Conclusion

Matthew Chapter Fifteen Verse Eleven challenges us profoundly regarding purity beyond mere outward appearances! Instead focusing inwardly transforming ourselves spiritually aligning completely wholeheartedly unto Almighty Creator thereby reflecting genuinely authentic righteous living outwardly glorifying Him eternally forevermore!

Chapter 5: Breaking Free from Rituals: Jesus' Challenge to Religious Legalism

Introduction: The Context of Matthew 15:11

In the Gospel of Matthew, chapter 15, Jesus confronts one of the most pervasive issues among the religious leaders of His time—legalism. Specifically, He addresses their obsession with man-made traditions that had been elevated to a status equal to or even above God's commandments. One such tradition was the ritual washing of hands before eating, which the Pharisees and scribes considered essential for maintaining ceremonial purity. However, in Matthew 15:11, Jesus makes a profound statement that shifts the focus from external rituals to internal purity: "It is not what goes into the mouth that defiles a person, but what comes out of the mouth; this defiles a person."

This chapter will explore how Jesus challenged these legalistic practices and redirected attention to God's commandments, emphasizing internal transformation over external conformity.

The Pharisees' Obsession with Rituals

The Pharisees were deeply committed to preserving Jewish traditions and laws. Over time, they developed an extensive set of oral traditions—later codified in texts like the Mishnah—that went beyond the written Law of Moses. These traditions included detailed rules about ceremonial handwashing before meals, which were intended to prevent ritual impurity.

In Matthew 15:1-2, we see this obsession in action: "Then Pharisees and scribes came to Jesus from Jerusalem and said, 'Why do your disciples break the tradition of the elders? For they do not wash their hands when they eat.'" This question reveals their priorities—they were more concerned with adherence to human traditions than with understanding God's heart behind His commandments.

The ritual handwashing itself was not inherently wrong; it was symbolic of spiritual cleanliness. However, by elevating this practice to a divine mandate, the Pharisees distorted its purpose. They used it as a measure of righteousness and excluded those who did not conform.

Jesus' Response: Exposing Hypocrisy

Jesus does not shy away from addressing their misplaced priorities. Instead of defending His disciples' actions directly, He turns the question back on the Pharisees and exposes their hypocrisy. In Matthew 15:3-6, He says:

"And why do you break the commandment of God for the sake of your tradition? For God commanded, 'Honor your father and your mother,' and 'Whoever reviles father or mother must surely die.' But you say, 'If anyone tells his father or his mother, "What you would have gained from me is given to God," he need not honor his father.' So, for the sake of your tradition you have made void the word of God."

Here, Jesus highlights how their man-made traditions actually led them to violate God's commandments. The specific example He cites involves a practice known as Corban, where individuals could dedicate their possessions to God as an offering while still retaining control over them during their lifetime. This loophole allowed people to avoid using those resources to care for their aging parents—a direct violation of the commandment to honor one's father and mother.

By pointing out this inconsistency, Jesus reveals that their legalism was not rooted in genuine devotion but in self-righteousness and pride.

The Heart Over Rituals

After exposing their hypocrisy, Jesus delivers a powerful teaching that redefines what it means to be clean or

23

unclean in God's eyes. In Matthew 15:10-11, He says:

"Hear and understand: it is not what goes into the mouth that defiles a person, but what comes out of the mouth; this defiles a person."

This statement would have been shocking to His audience because it directly challenged centuries-old dietary laws and purity codes. However, Jesus was not abolishing these laws outright; rather, He was revealing their ultimate purpose—to point toward inner holiness rather than mere external compliance.

Jesus explains further in verses 18-20: "But what comes out of the mouth proceeds from the heart, and this defiles a person. For out of the heart come evil thoughts, murder, adultery, sexual immorality, theft, false witness, slander. These are what defile a person. But to eat with unwashed hands does not defile anyone."

Here lies one of Jesus' central teachings about true spirituality: righteousness begins in the heart. External rituals cannot purify a corrupt heart; only genuine repentance and faith can lead to transformation.

Breaking Free from Legalism

Jesus' confrontation with legalism in Matthew 15 serves as both a warning and an invitation for us today. Legalism often begins with good intentions—a desire to honor God through obedience—but it can quickly devolve into prideful rule-keeping that misses the heart of worship.

Warning Against Elevating Traditions

One key lesson from this passage is that we must be cautious about elevating human traditions or preferences above Scripture. Just as the Pharisees turned handwashing into an essential act of righteousness, modern believers can fall into similar traps by insisting on extra-biblical rules or practices as measures of spirituality.

For example:

Insisting on specific styles of worship music.

Judging others based on dress codes or outward appearances.

Equating church attendance or participation in certain programs with spiritual maturity.

While these practices may have value in certain contexts, they should never replace or overshadow God's clear commands.

Embracing Internal Transformation

Breaking free from legalism requires shifting our focus from external conformity to internal transformation. As Vlad Ciolan notes in his reflections on legalism, true spirituality is about cultivating love for God and others through faith in Christ—not merely adhering to rules for fear of condemnation.

Paul echoes this idea in Romans 14:17: "For the kingdom of God is not a matter of eating and drinking but of righteousness and peace and joy in the Holy Spirit." Our relationship with God is defined by grace through faith (Ephesians 2:8-9), not by our ability to keep every rule perfectly.

Conclusion: Living Out True Freedom

Jesus' challenge to religious legalism calls us back to authentic worship rooted in love for God rather than fear-driven rule-following. By prioritizing internal transformation over external rituals:

We honor God's commandments without adding unnecessary burdens.

We experience freedom from guilt and shame imposed by man-made standards.

We reflect Christ's character more fully as we grow in love for Him and others.

As we meditate on Matthew 15:11— "It is not what goes

into the mouth that defiles a person…"—let us examine our own hearts for traces of legalism or misplaced priorities. May we seek true holiness through faith in Christ alone while extending grace toward others who are also on this journey toward freedom.

Chapter 6: From Clean Hands to Clean Hearts: Redefining Spiritual Purity

Introduction: The Shift from External to Internal Purity

The sixth chapter of Apostle Bill Amor's book, Matt 15:11, titled "From Clean Hands to Clean Hearts: Redefining Spiritual Purity," explores a profound shift in the understanding of spiritual cleanliness. Rooted in Jesus' teaching in Matthew 15:11— "It is not what goes into the mouth that defiles a person, but what comes out of the mouth; this defiles a person"—this chapter contrasts the Old Testament ceremonial laws with Jesus' emphasis on moral purity. Under the New Covenant, Jesus redefined what it means to be spiritually clean by moving beyond external rituals and focusing on the condition of the heart.

To fully grasp this transformation, we must first examine the Old Testament framework for purity and then explore how Jesus challenged and fulfilled these concepts through His teachings and actions.

Old Testament Ceremonial Laws: A Focus on External Purity

In the Old Testament, ceremonial laws played a central role in defining purity. These laws were given as part of God's covenant with Israel and were designed to set His people apart as holy. They encompassed various aspects of life, including dietary restrictions (Leviticus 11), ritual washings (Exodus 30:17-21), and regulations concerning contact with unclean objects or individuals (Numbers 19). For example:

Dietary Laws: Certain foods were deemed "clean" or "unclean." Leviticus 11 outlines specific animals that could be eaten (e.g., those that chew cud and have split hooves) versus those that were forbidden (e.g., pigs and shellfish). These dietary restrictions symbolized separation from pagan nations and obedience to God's commands.

Ritual Washings: Priests were required to wash their hands and feet before entering the Tabernacle or offering sacrifices (Exodus 30:19-21). This act symbolized purification before approaching God's holy presence.

Avoidance of Impurity: Contact with certain things—such as dead bodies, leprosy, or bodily discharges—rendered individuals ceremonially unclean (Leviticus 15). Such individuals had to undergo purification rituals before rejoining communal worship.

These laws emphasized external actions as a means of maintaining holiness. However, they also pointed to humanity's deeper need for spiritual cleansing—a theme that would find its ultimate fulfillment in Christ.

Jesus' Radical Teaching on Purity

When Jesus began His ministry, He confronted the Pharisees and religious leaders who had elevated these external rituals above their intended purpose. In Matthew 15:1-20, Jesus directly challenged their obsession with ceremonial handwashing:

"Why do you break the commandment of God for the sake of your tradition? ... It is not what goes into the mouth that defiles a person, but what comes out of the mouth; this defiles a person." (Matthew 15:3, 11)

Here, Jesus shifted the focus from outward compliance to inward transformation. He declared that true defilement comes not from eating certain foods but from sinful thoughts and actions originating in the heart:

"For out of the heart come evil thoughts—murder, adultery, sexual immorality, theft, false testimony, slander." (Matthew 15:19)

This teaching was revolutionary because it redefined purity as an issue of moral character rather than ritual observance. By doing so, Jesus exposed hypocrisy among religious leaders who appeared outwardly righteous but harbored corruption within their hearts (Matthew 23:25-28).

Fulfillment of Ceremonial Laws in Christ

Jesus did not abolish the Old Testament law; rather, He fulfilled it (Matthew 5:17). The ceremonial laws served as shadows pointing toward Him—the ultimate source of spiritual cleansing:

Dietary Laws Fulfilled: In Mark 7:18-19 (a parallel passage to Matthew 15), Mark adds an editorial note explaining that Jesus declared all foods clean. This signified that dietary restrictions were no longer necessary under the New Covenant because Christ's sacrifice made believers spiritually pure.

Ritual Washings Superseded: The physical act of washing hands or utensils was replaced by spiritual cleansing through faith in Christ. As Hebrews 10:22 states, "Let us draw near to God with a sincere heart and with full assurance that faith brings, having our hearts sprinkled to cleanse us from a guilty conscience."

Purification Through Christ's Blood: The sacrifices required for purification under Mosaic Law foreshadowed Christ's atoning death on the cross. His blood cleanses believers from all sin once and for all (Hebrews 9:13-14).

Through His life, death, and resurrection, Jesus inaugurated a new way for humanity to approach God—not through external rituals but through repentance and faith.

Moral Purity Under the New Covenant

Under the New Covenant established by Christ, moral purity takes precedence over ceremonial observance. This does not mean that God no longer cares about holiness; rather, He calls believers to pursue righteousness from within:

Purity of Heart: In Matthew 5:8, Jesus proclaimed in His Sermon on the Mount, "Blessed are the pure in heart, for they shall see God." True purity begins with an undivided devotion to God—a heart free from hypocrisy and sin.

Transformation by Grace: Unlike Old Testament laws that relied on human effort for compliance, New Covenant purity is achieved through grace. Titus 2:11-12 teaches that God's grace trains believers "to renounce ungodliness" and live upright lives.

The Role of Love: Paul emphasized love as central to Christian morality under the New Covenant (Romans 13:8-10). Love fulfills God's law because it seeks others' good rather than selfish gain—a stark contrast to legalistic rule-following.

By redefining spiritual cleanliness as an internal reality shaped by love and grace rather than external conformity to rules alone—Jesus elevated moral purity above mere rituals

Conclusion

In redefining spiritual purity from clean hands to clean hearts under the New Covenant framework—Jesus transformed humanity's relationship with God forevermore! While Old Testament ceremonial laws highlighted mankind's neediness & separation due-to-sinfulness-Christ bridged-that-gap entirely enabling direct access via inward renewal empowered-by-Holy-Spirit!

Chapter 7: Food for Thought: The End of Dietary Laws in Light of Christ's Teaching

Introduction: The Context of Matthew 15:11

In Matthew 15:11, Jesus makes a profound statement that challenges the traditional Jewish understanding of purity laws: "It is not what goes into the mouth that defiles a person, but what comes out of the mouth; this defiles a person." At first glance, this declaration appears to undermine centuries of dietary restrictions outlined in the Mosaic Law. These laws, detailed in Leviticus 11 and Deuteronomy 14, were central to Jewish identity and religious practice. However, Jesus' teaching here is not merely about food; it is about redefining the concept of holiness and purity under the New Covenant.

To understand how Matthew 15:11 foreshadows the end of Old Testament dietary laws, we must examine its theological implications and how it aligns with later revelations, particularly Peter's vision in Acts 10. This chapter will explore these connections step by step.

Step 1: Understanding the Purpose of Old Testament Dietary Laws

The dietary laws given to Israel served several purposes:

Holiness and Separation: Leviticus 20:25-26 emphasizes that these laws set Israel apart as God's holy people. By abstaining from certain foods deemed "unclean," Israelites demonstrated their distinctiveness from surrounding nations.

Symbolism of Purity: The distinction between clean and unclean animals symbolized moral and spiritual purity. It reminded Israel to remain pure in their relationship with God.

31

Covenantal Identity: Observing dietary restrictions was a visible sign of Israel's covenant with Yahweh.

However, these laws were never intended as an end in themselves. They pointed forward to a greater reality—the coming of Christ—who would fulfill the law (Matthew 5:17) and establish a new covenant based on faith rather than ritual observance.

Step 2: Jesus' Radical Teaching in Matthew 15

In Matthew 15, Jesus confronts Pharisaic traditions that prioritized external rituals over internal righteousness. The immediate context involves a dispute over handwashing before meals—a tradition not mandated by Mosaic Law but added by rabbinic authorities (Matthew 15:1-2). In response, Jesus shifts the focus from external actions to internal character:

He rebukes the Pharisees for elevating human traditions above God's commandments (Matthew 15:3-9).

He declares that true defilement comes not from eating certain foods but from sinful thoughts and actions originating in the heart (Matthew 15:18-20).

By stating that "what goes into someone's mouth does not defile them" (Matthew 15:11), Jesus begins to dismantle the notion that dietary restrictions are essential for maintaining spiritual purity. Instead, He emphasizes moral integrity and inner transformation as markers of true holiness.

Step 3: Acts 10—Peter's Vision and Its Implications

The full abolition of dietary laws becomes explicit in Acts 10 through Peter's vision. While praying on a rooftop, Peter sees a sheet descending from heaven containing all kinds of animals—both clean and unclean—and hears a voice commanding him to "kill and eat" (Acts 10:13). Peter initially resists, citing his adherence to Jewish dietary laws (Acts 10:14). However, God responds decisively: "What God has made clean, do not call common" (Acts 10:15).

This vision is repeated three times for emphasis, signaling

its importance. Later, Peter interprets its meaning when he meets Cornelius, a Gentile centurion:

Peter realizes that the vision symbolizes God's acceptance of Gentiles into His covenant community without requiring adherence to Jewish ceremonial laws (Acts 10:28).

He proclaims that "God shows no partiality" and grants salvation to all who believe in Christ (Acts 10:34-35).

Thus, Acts 10 confirms what Jesus hinted at in Matthew 15 —that external rituals like dietary restrictions are no longer necessary under the New Covenant.

Step 4: Theological Significance Under the New Covenant

The abolition of dietary laws reflects broader theological truths about Christ's work:

Fulfillment of the Law:

Jesus fulfilled all aspects of the Mosaic Law—moral, ceremonial, and civil—through His life, death, and resurrection (Romans 8:3-4). As Paul writes in Romans 10:4, "Christ is the end [Greek 'telos,' meaning goal or fulfillment] of the law for righteousness to everyone who believes."

By fulfilling these requirements on behalf of humanity, Christ rendered obsolete practices like dietary restrictions that symbolized separation from sin.

Universal Salvation:

Under the Old Covenant, dietary laws reinforced Israel's distinctiveness as God's chosen people. However, under the New Covenant inaugurated by Christ's blood (Luke 22:20), salvation extends universally to Jews and Gentiles alike.

Ephesians 2 explains how Christ broke down "the dividing wall" between Jews and Gentiles by abolishing commandments expressed in ordinances (Ephesians 2:14-

16).

Spiritual Purity Over Ritual Purity:

Jesus' teaching prioritizes inward transformation over outward conformity. As Paul states in Colossians 2:16-17, food regulations were merely shadows pointing to Christ—the substance belongs to Him.

True purity now comes through faith in Christ and living according to His Spirit rather than adhering to external rules.

Step-by-Step Connection Between Matthew 15 and Acts 10

In Matthew 15:11:

Jesus introduces a revolutionary idea—that food itself cannot defile because defilement originates from within.

This teaching lays groundwork for understanding purity as an internal matter rather than an external one tied to ritual observance.

In Acts 10:

God explicitly declares all foods clean through Peter's vision while simultaneously revealing His plan for Gentile inclusion.

This event fulfills Jesus' earlier teaching by demonstrating that distinctions based on ceremonial law are no longer relevant under grace.

Together, these passages reveal how Christ redefined holiness under His New Covenant—a shift from legalistic observance toward faith-based righteousness accessible to all people.

Conclusion

Matthew 15 foreshadows one of Christianity's most transformative truths—that salvation is no longer bound by ceremonial practices like dietary restrictions but is freely available through faith in Christ alone. By declaring that food cannot defile us spiritually (Matthew 15) and later confirming this truth through Peter's vision (Acts 10), Scripture underscores God's ultimate plan for humanity's redemption—a plan rooted not in external rituals but in internal renewal through His Son.

As believers today reflect on these passages, we are reminded that our relationship with God hinges not on what we eat but on who we trust—Jesus Christ—the One who fulfilled every requirement of the law so we might live freely under grace.

Chapter 8: Guarding Your Words: The Power of Speech in Spiritual Life

Introduction: The Weight of Our Words

In Matthew 15:11, Jesus declares, "It is not what goes into the mouth that defiles a person, but what comes out of the mouth; this defiles a person." This profound statement shifts the focus from external rituals to the internal condition of the heart, as revealed by our words. Speech is not merely a tool for communication; it is a reflection of our spiritual state and has immense power to shape our lives and the lives of others. In this chapter, we will explore practical ways to guard our words and harness their potential to build up rather than tear down.

The Dual Power of Speech: Building or Defiling

Proverbs 18:21 reminds us, "Death and life are in the power of the tongue." This duality underscores that speech can either edify or harm. Words have the capacity to:

Build Up: Encouraging, comforting, and inspiring others aligns with God's will for how we should use our speech (Ephesians 4:29). For instance, speaking words of affirmation can strengthen relationships and foster trust.

Defile: Gossip, lies, harsh criticism, or unkind remarks can damage reputations, relationships, and even one's own spiritual health (James 3:6).

Understanding this dual nature compels us to approach speech with intentionality and reverence.

Practical Applications for Guarding Your Words

1. Pause Before Speaking

James 1:19 advises believers to be "quick to listen, slow to speak." Pausing before responding allows time to consider whether your words are necessary and beneficial. Ask yourself:

Is what I am about to say true?

Will my words uplift or do harm?

Would I want someone else to say this about me?

This momentary pause can prevent impulsive remarks that might later lead to regret.

2. Speak with Intentionality

Intentional speech involves choosing words that align with God's truth. Ephesians 4:29 instructs us: "Let no corrupting talk come out of your mouths, but only such as is good for building up." To practice intentionality:

Replace complaints with gratitude.

Use affirmations instead of criticisms.

Share Scripture or godly wisdom when appropriate.

By focusing on edification rather than destruction, you reflect Christ's love in your interactions.

3. Guard Against Gossip

Proverbs 16:28 warns that gossip "separates close friends." Gossip often stems from pride or insecurity and serves no constructive purpose. To avoid gossip:

Refuse to participate in conversations that demean others.

Redirect discussions toward positive topics.

Pray for those who are being spoken about negatively.

Eliminating gossip from your speech fosters peace and unity within your community.

4. Practice Active Listening

Listening well is an essential component of guarding your

words. Proverbs 18:13 states: "If one gives an answer before he hears, it is his folly and shame." Active listening involves:

Giving full attention to the speaker without interrupting.

Seeking clarification before responding.

Empathizing with their perspective.

When you listen attentively, you are less likely to respond hastily or insensitively.

5. Rely on the Holy Spirit

Self-control is a fruit of the Spirit (Galatians 5:22–23), making reliance on God essential for mastering your tongue. Pray daily for guidance over your speech using verses like Psalm 141:3: "Set a guard over my mouth, Lord; keep watch over the door of my lips."

The Holy Spirit empowers believers to speak wisely and lovingly even in challenging situations.

The Heart-Speech Connection

Jesus teaches in Luke 6:45 that "out of the abundance of the heart his mouth speaks." This connection between heart and speech highlights that controlling one's words begins with addressing internal attitudes such as pride, anger, or bitterness. To cultivate a heart aligned with God:

Meditate on Scripture regularly (Psalm 119:11).

Confess sins related to harmful speech (1 John 1:9).

Seek transformation through prayer (Ezekiel 36:26).

A purified heart naturally produces pure speech.

Consequences of Uncontrolled Speech

Failing to guard one's words can lead to significant consequences:

Damaged Relationships: Harsh or careless remarks erode

trust and intimacy.

Spiritual Decay: Negative speech grieves the Holy Spirit (Ephesians 4:30) and hinders spiritual growth.

Loss of Witness: Unwholesome talk undermines credibility as a follower of Christ (Colossians 4:6).

Recognizing these consequences motivates believers to take their speech seriously.

Benefits of Guarded Speech

Conversely, guarding your words yields numerous blessings:

Stronger Relationships: Kindness fosters trust and deepens connections.

Inner Peace: Avoiding conflict through wise speech brings tranquility (Proverbs 15:1).

Spiritual Growth: Aligning your words with God's truth strengthens faith (Philippians 4:8).

By choosing life-giving words consistently, you become an instrument for God's purposes.

Practical Exercises for Daily Practice

Exercise #1 – The "Three Gates" Test

Before speaking, pass your thoughts through three gates:

Is it true?

Is it kind?

Is it necessary?

Only proceed if all three criteria are met.

Exercise #2 – Daily Reflection

At the end of each day:

Reflect on moments where your words built someone up.

Identify instances where you could have spoken more wisely. Pray for forgiveness where needed and ask God for strength moving forward.

Exercise #3 – Memorize Key Scriptures

Commit verses like Proverbs 18:21 or James 1:19–20 to memory so they guide you in moments when you're tempted toward harmful speech.

Conclusion

Guarding your words is both a spiritual discipline and an act of obedience rooted in love for God and others. By pausing before speaking, practicing intentionality, avoiding gossip, listening actively, relying on the Holy Spirit, and cultivating a pure heart, you align yourself with Christ's example as described in Matthew 15:11—choosing not defilement but edification through every word spoken.

May we all strive daily toward using our tongues as instruments for blessing rather than harm so that our lives reflect His glory in every conversation we have!

Conclusion

In conclusion, the teaching based on Matthew 15:11 (AMP) emphasizes that true spiritual purity and honor before God are not determined by external practices, such as dietary laws or ceremonial rituals, but by the condition of one's heart and the words that flow from it. Jesus' message redirects focus from outward appearances to inward transformation, urging believers to cultivate integrity, kindness, and righteousness in their thoughts and speech. This teaching serves as a reminder that our words have immense power—they can either reflect a heart aligned with God's will or reveal inner corruption. Therefore, followers of Christ are called to examine their hearts continually and ensure that what comes out of their mouths glorifies God and edifies others.

www.ingramcontent.com/pod-product-compliance
Lightning Source LLC
Chambersburg PA
CBHW071225130626
46555CB00004B/1850